365 Jokes for Kids

by Chrissy Voeg

PHILADELPHIA PA

Philadelphia PA

ISBN 978-0-9850564-6-9

Printed in the United States of America

CHAPTER 1

A Joke for Every Day of the Year

1.

Q: How do you make a tissue dance?

A: You put a boogie in it!

2.

Q: What do you call a witch at the beach?

A. A SandWich!

3.

Q: What can you catch but not throw?

A: A cold.

4.

Q: What happens when you tell an egg a joke?

A: It cracks up!

5.

Q: Why is 8 afraid of 7?

A: Because 7-8-9.

6.

Q: Why didn't the skeleton cross the road?

A: Because he didn't have the guts to do it.

7.

Q: What did the nose say to the finger?

A: Stop picking on me.

8.

Q: What did one man say to another man with a mustache?

A. I mustache you a question.

9.

Q: What do you call a fish that won't share?

A: SHELL-fish.

10.

Q: Where is a rabbit's favorite place to eat?

A: IHOP.

11.

Q: What do witches study in school?

A: Spelling.

12.

Q: What do you get when you cross a vampire with a snowman?

A. Frostbite.

13.

Q: Why didn't the skeleton go to the dance?

A: He had no-BODY to go with

14.

Q: What's a ghost's favorite dessert?

A: Boo-berry pie.

15.

Q: What has four wheels and flies?

A: A garbage truck.

16.

Q: How do you catch a squirrel?

A: Climb a tree and act like a nut.

17.

Knock knock.

Who's there?

Hatch.

Hatch Who?

Bless you!

18.

Knock knock.

Who's there?

Lettuce.

Lettuce who?

Lettuce in its freezing out here!

19.

Q: What word gets shorter when you add 2 letters to it?

A: Short.

20.

Q: What has 4 eyes but can't see?

A: Mississippi.

21.

Q: What can you hear but not touch or see?

A: Your voice.

22.

Q: What kind of band can't play music?

A: A rubber band.

23.

Q: I'm full of keys but can't open any door, what am I?

A: A piano.

24.

Q: I can't speak or hear, but I'll always tell the truth, what am I?

A: A mirror.

25.

Q: What can you break without touching or seeing?

A: A promise.

26.

Q: Everyone has it and no one can lose it, what is it?

A: A shadow.

27.

Q: I am a vehicle that is spelled the same backwards and forwards, what am I?

A: RACE CAR.

28.

Q: What building has the most stories?

A: A library.

29.

Q: What are 2 things that you can never eat for breakfast?

A: Lunch and Dinner.

30.

Q: What number do you get when you multiply all the numbers on a calculator?

A: 0.

31.

Q: Wanna hear a pizza joke?

A: Nevermind, it's too cheesy.

32.

Q: What room can't you walk into?

A: A mushroom.

33.

Q: Why did the student eat her homework?

A: Because the teacher said it was a piece of cake.

34.

Q: What goes over your head and under your feet?

A: A jump rope.

35.

Q: Who can hold up a bus with one hand?

A: A crossing guard.

36.

Q: Why did the pie go to the dentist?

A: It needed a filling.

37.

Q: What kind of mistake does a ghost make?

A: A boo-boo.

38.

Knock, knock

Who's there?

Dismay

Dismay who?

Dismay be a joke but it's not that funny.

39.

Knock knock.

Who's there?

A herd.

A herd who?

A herd you were home so I came right over.

40.

Q: What do you get when you cross an octopus with a mouse?

A: A squeaktopus.

41.

Q: Why was the baseball player arrested?

A: Because he stole second base.

42.

A: What travels around the world but stays in a corner?

A: A stamp.

43.

Q: What's black and white and read all over?

A: A newspaper.

44.

Q: Why did the pig become an actor?

A: Because he was a ham.

45.

Q: Where does a 2,000 pound gorilla sit?

A: Anywhere it wants.

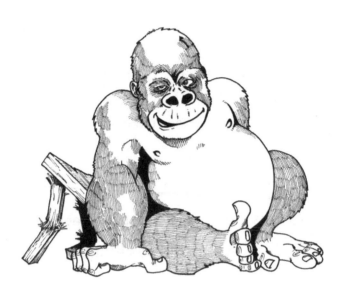

46.

Knock, knock.

Who's there?

Wooden shoe.

Wooden shoe who?

Wooden shoe like to hear another joke?

47.

Knock Knock.

Who's there?

Boo!

Boo who?

Don't cry, it's just a joke!

48.

Q: What goes up and down and doesn't move?

A: The stairs.

49.

Q: How can you name three consecutive days without saying "Wednesday", "Thursday", or "Friday"?

A: Yesterday, today, tomorrow.

50.

Q: How did Ben Franklin feel after he discovered electricity?

A: Shocked.

51.

Q: What did Mars say to Saturn?

A: Give me a ring sometime.

52.

Q: What kinds of books do bunnies like?

A: Ones with hoppy endings.

53.

Q: Where do you find a chicken with no legs?

A: Wherever you left it.

54.

Q: Why can't a tyrannosaurus rex clap?

A: They are extinct.

55.

Knock knock.

Who's there?

Banana.

Banana who?

Knock knock.

Who's there?

Banana.

Banana who?

Knock knock.

Who's there?

Banana.

Banana who?

Knock knock.

Who's there?

Orange.

Orange who?

Orange you glad I didn't say banana?

56.

Q: Why can't you hear a pterodactyl going to the bathroom?

A: Because the pee is silent!

57.

Q: What can run, but cannot walk?

A: Your nose.

58.

Q: What does one egg say to the other egg?

A: You crack me up!

59.

Q: What do you call a monkey with a banana in each ear?

A: Anything you want, it can't hear you.

60.

Q: What is a cat on a beach called?

A. Sandy Claws.

61.

Q: What goes up but never comes down?

A: Your age.

62.

Q: What asks but never answers?

A: An owl.

63.

Q: What do a baker and a millionaire have in common?

A: They're both rolling in dough.

64.

Q: Why can't skeletons play church music?

A: Because they have no organs.

65.

Q: What animal can jump higher than a building?

A: All of them – buildings can't jump!

66.

Q: Why do birds fly south in the winter?

A: Because it's too far to walk.

67.

Q: Where do cows go on a date?

A: To the moooovies.

68.

Q: What starts with T, ends with T, and is filled with T?

A: A Teapot.

69.

Q: Which weighs more a pound of marshmallows or a pound of rocks?

A: Neither – they both weigh a pound.

70.

Q: What starts with E ends with E and has only one letter?

A: An envelope.

71.

Q: There were two elephants and a giraffe under one umbrella. Why didn't they get wet?

A: It wasn't raining!

72.

Q: What's the best time to go to the dentist?

A: At tooth-hurty.

73.

Q: A truck driver is going the wrong way down a one way street. A police officer sees him but does not stop him. Why?

A: The truck driver was walking.

74.

Q: A man is out in the pouring rain. He isn't wearing a hat or carrying an umbrella. His clothes are completely soaked through but not a single hair on his head is wet. How is that possible?

A: He is bald!

75.

Q: Why did the chewing gum cross the road?

A: Because it was stuck to the chicken's foot.

76.

Q: Why was the chicken afraid of the chicken?

A: It was a chicken!

77.

Q: Why did the clown go to the doctor?

A: Because he was feeling a little funny.

78.

Q: Why did the cookies go to the doctor?

A: They were feeling crummy.

79.

Q: What type of horses only go out at night?

A: Nightmares.

80.

Q: What goes zzub zzub?

A: A bee flying backwards.

81.

Q: Which side of the cat has more fur?

A: The outside.

82.

Q: What do you call a bear with no teeth?

A: A gummy bear.

83.

Q: What has 18 legs and catches flies?

A: A baseball team.

84.

Q: What do you call a boomerang that won't come back?

A: A stick.

85.

Q: How do you know your clock is crazy?

A: It goes cuckoo.

86.

Q: What's even smarter than a talking bird?

A: A spelling bee.

87.

Q: Where does Friday come before Monday?

A: In the dictionary.

88.

Q: How can you make seven even?

A: Remove the S.

89.

Q: What does the winner of the race lose?

A: His breath.

90.

Q: What goes tick tick woof woof?

A: A watch dog

91.

Q: What's a boxer's favorite drink?

A: Punch!

92.

Q: What is only a small box but can weigh over a hundred pounds?

A: A scale.

93.

Q: What do you call a dog on the beach in the summer?

A: A hot dog.

94.

Q: Where do pencils come from?

A: Pencil-vania.

95.

Q: How does a witch tell time?

A: With her witch watch.

96.

Q: What's the problem with twin witches?

A: You can't tell which witch is which.

97.

Knock knock.

Who's there?

Owls say.

Owls say who?

Yep.

98.

Knock knock.

Who's there?

Little old lady.

Little old lady who?

Wow, I didn't know you could yodel!

99.

Q: What did the hat say to the scarf?

A: You hang around while I go on ahead.

100.

Q: What does a snail say when its riding on a turtle's back?

A: Wheeeeeee!!!

101.

Q: What does one volcano say to the other?

A: I lava you.

102.

Q: What did the fruit tree say to the farmer?

A: Stop picking on me!

103.

Q: What's black and white, black and white, black and white?

A: A penguin rolling down a hill.

104.

Q: What has 40 feet and sings?

A: A 20 person choir.

105.

Q: What runs but can't walk?

A: The kitchen sink.

106.

Q: What is a button that won't unbutton?

A: Bellybutton.

107.

Q: What do you call the hippie's wife?

A: Mississippi.

108.

Q: Why didn't the 2 4's want dinner?

A: Because they already had 8.

109.

Q: What did 0 say to 8?

A: Nice belt.

110.

Q: What goes around the yard and never stops?

A: A fence.

111.

Q: What do you call a 200-year-old ant?

A: An ANTique.

112.

Q: Why are snakes hard to fool?

A: You can't pull their leg.

113.

Q: What key won't open any door?

A: A turkey.

114.

Q: What does a clock do when it's hungry?

A: Goes back 4 seconds.

115.

Q: Which month has 28 days?

A: All of them.

116.

Q: Why was the strawberry crying?

A: Because his parents were in a jam.

117.

Q: What do you call a chicken at the North Pole?

A: Lost.

118.

Q: Why do spirits make bad liars?

A: Because you can see right through them.

119.

Q: What is the mouse's favorite desert?

A: Cheesecake.

120.

Knock knock.

Who's there?

Cowsgo.

Cowsgo who?

No they don't, cows go moo.

121.

Knock knock.

Who's there?

Abby.

Abby who?

Abby birthday to you!

122.

Knock, knock.

Who's there?

Tank.

Tank who?

You're welcome!

123.

Knock, knock.

Who's there?

Howard.

Howard who?

Howard I know?

124.

Knock, knock.

Who's there?

Figs.

Figs who?

Figs the doorbell, its broken!

125.

Knock knock.

Who's there?

Doris.

Doris who?

Doris locked, that's why I knocked.

126.

Q: What can you hold without using your hands?

A: Your breath.

127.

Q: When is a door not a door?

A: When it's a jar.

128.

Q: What kind of driver never gets a ticket?

A: A screwdriver.

129.

Q: What's worse than finding a worm in your apple?

A: Finding half a worm in your apple.

130.

Q: What do dogs have that no other animals have?

A: Puppies.

131.

Q: What's the biggest ant in the world?

A: An elephant.

132.

Q: Why do seagulls fly over the sea?

A: Because if they flew over the bay they'd be bagels.

133.

Q: Why did the turkey cross the road twice?

A: To prove he wasn't chicken.

134.

Q: Someone said you sounded like an owl.

A: Who?

135.

Q: Why can't you trust atoms?

A: They make up everything.

136.

Q: Why are kindergarten teachers so good?

A: They make the little things count.

137.

Q: How are golf and donuts the same?

A: They both have a hole in one.

138.

Q: What has a bed that you can't sleep in?

A: A river.

139.

Q: What does the egg like to do for fun?

A: Kara-yolk-ee.

140.

Q: What does a bug detective do for a living?

A: Infestigate.

141.

Q: What's an owl's favorite mystery?

A: A whooooo- done-it.

142.

Knock knock.

Who's there?

Irish.

Irish who?

Irish you a happy St. Patrick's Day!

143.

Knock, knock.

Who's there?

Ya.

Ya who?

I'm excited to see you too!

144.

Knock, knock.

Who's there?

A broken pencil.

A broken pencil who?

Oh never mind, it's pointless.

145.

Knock, knock

Who's there?

Frank.

Frank who?

Frank you for being my friend.

146.

Q: What do you call cheese that's not yours?

A: Nacho cheese.

147.

Q: What did the man say to his tie?

A: Stop hanging on me.

148.

Q: What did one grapevine say to another?

A: Stop wining!

149.

Q: What did the person say to the star?

A: Stop spacing out.

150.

Q: How do you stop a buffalo from charging?

A: Take away his credit card.

151.

Q: What do you call a bull that's asleep?

A: A bulldozer.

152.

Q: When is it bad luck to see a black cat?

A: When you're a mouse.

153.

Q: What kind of ant is good at math?

A: AccountANT.

154.

Q: What do you get from a pampered cow?

A: Spoiled milk.

155.

Q: What does a cat say when you step on its tail?

A: Me-OW!

156.

Q: What do you call a fish without an eye?

A: Fsh.

157.

Q: What did the gorilla say to the lion when he was hungry?

A: Gorilla me a hamburger!!

158.

Q: What do you call an alligator wearing a vest?

A: An investigator.

159.

Q: What did the turkey say to the pig?

A: You're bacon me hungry!

160.

Q: What does a nut say when it sneezes?

A: Cashew!

161.

Q: What do you call a bear with no ears?

A: B.

162.

Q: What do elves learn in school?

A: The elf-a-bet.

163.

Q: Why did the golfer wear two pairs of pants?

A: In case he got a hole in one.

164.

Q: Where do cars go for a swim?

A: A car pool.

165.

Q: Where do generals keep their armies?

A: In their sleevies.

166.

Q: What's the difference between a fly and superman?

A: Superman can fly but a fly can't superman.

167.

Q: How can you tell the psychiatrist from the patients on the ward?

A: The psychiatrist has the keys to the door.

168.

Q: Why did the sea monster eat 5 ships full of potatoes?

A: Because nobody can eat just one potato ship.

169.

Q: Why did the boy put candy under his pillow?

A: Because he wanted sweet dreams.

170.

Q: When do you go on red and stop on green?

A: When you're eating watermelon.

171.

Q: What does a piece of toast wear to bed?

A: Jammies!

172.

Q: What do you give a lemon in distress?

A: Lemon-aide.

173.

Q: What did one grape say to another?

A: Stop hanging around me.

174.

Q: Where can you find an ocean with no water?

A: On a map.

175.

Q: If a yellow house is yellow and a blue house is blue, what color is a green house?

A: Clear – a greenhouse is made of glass.

176.

Q: Why do you always have to go to bed?

A: Because your bed won't come to you.

177.

Q: What kind of table has no legs?

A: A multiplication table.

178.

Q: What did the judge say when the skunk ran into the courtroom?

A: Odor in the court!

179.

Q: What do you call a sheep with no legs?

A: A cloud.

180.

Q: What can you put in a barrel to make it lighter?

A: Holes.

181.

Q: Why didn't the boy take the bus home?

A: Because his mother would have made him take it back.

182.

Q: What did Dracula go to the doctor?

A: He couldn't stop coffin.

183.

Q: Why was the longest human nose only 11 inches?

A: If it was 12 inches it would be a foot!

184.

Q: Hey is your refrigerator running?

A: You better go catch it!

185.

Q: What's black and white and red all over?

A: A sunburned zebra.

186.

Q: Where was the declaration of independence signed?

A: At the bottom.

187.

Q: What did the puzzle say to the last piece?

A: You complete me.

188.

Q: What has an eye but can't see?

A: A needle.

189.

Q: What kind of nails do carpenters hate hammering?

A: Fingernails.

190.

Q: Why was the math book depressed?

A: It had too many problems.

191.

Q: What did the triangle say to the circle?

A: You're pointless.

192.

Q: Why did the boy throw the clock out the window?

A: Because he wanted to see time fly.

193.

Q: Why is that brain so expensive?

A: Because it was never used!

194.

Q: Why don't skeletons get into fights?

A: They don't have the guts.

195.

Q: How do you make an egg roll?

A: Push it.

196.

Q: Why didn't the teddy bear eat his lunch?

A: Because he was stuffed.

197.

Q: Why do dogs run in circles?

A: Because it's too hard to run in squares.

198.

Q: What do you get when you cross a Rottweiler and a collie?

A: A dog that bites you, then goes for help.

199.

Q: What gives you the power and strength to walk through walls?

A: A door.

200.

Q: What do you call a shoe made from a banana?

A: A slipper.

201.

Q: What's the best way to talk to a monster?

A: From far away.

202.

Q: What has a hundred heads and a hundred tails?

A: One hundred pennies.

203.

Q: How do you get straight A's?

A: Use a ruler.

204.

Q: What 11 letter word is always spelled incorrectly?

A: Incorrectly.

205.

Q: What works only after it's been fired?

A: A rocket.

206.

Q: What do you call a skeleton who won't work?

A: Lazy bones.

207.

Q: How do you make a skeleton laugh?

A: Tickle its funny bone.

208.

Q: What did the skeleton order for dinner?

A: Spare ribs.

209.

Q: What do you call witches who live together?

A: Broom mates.

210.

Q: What has a bottom at the top?

A: Your legs.

211.

Q: What room is useless for a ghost?

A: A living room.

212.

Q: If you had 7 apples in one hand and 6 oranges in the other hand, what would you have?

A: Really big hands.

213.

A: What kind of bow can't be tied?

A: A rainbow.

214.

Q: Why did the man keep doing the backstroke?

A: Because he just ate and didn't want to swim on a full stomach.

215.

Q: What washes up on small beaches?

A: Microwaves.

216.

Q: What race is never run?

A: A swimming race.

217.

Q: Why did the cantaloupe jump into the lake?

A: Because it wanted to be a watermelon.

218.

Q: How do you make a fire with 2 sticks?

A: Make sure you have a match.

219.

Q: How do you make a witch itch?

A: Take away her W.

220.

Q: What's black and white and red all over?

A: An embarrassed mime.

221.

Q: Why do cows wear bells?

A: Because their horns don't work.

222.

Q: How did the barber win the race?

A: He knew a short cut.

223.

Q: What is a woodpecker's favorite joke?

A: A knock knock joke.

224.

Q: What is always coming soon but never arrives?

A: Tomorrow.

225.

Q: Why did the tomato blush?

A: It saw the salad dressing.

226.

Q: What did one hat on the hat rack say to the other?

A: You stay here and I'll go on ahead.

227.

Q: What did the digital clock say to the grandfather clock?

A: Look grandpa – no hands!

228.

Q: What did the baby corn say to the mama corn?

A: Where's the popcorn?

229.

Q: How does the ocean say hello?

A: It waves.

230.

Patient: "Doctor, I get heartburn whenever I eat birthday cake."

Doctor: "Did you try removing the candles first?"

231.

Q: What gets smaller as it gets older?

A: A candle.

232.

Q: I run but can't walk, what am I?

A: A river.

233.

Q: What has 4 fingers and a thumb but is not alive?

A: A glove.

234.

Q: A girl is alone in a completely dark house with no electricity and no candles or lanterns. It is night and she is reading. How?

A: She is blind and reading braille.

235.

Q: How many seconds are there in a year?

A: Twelve.
January 2, February 2, March 2, April 2, May 2, June 2, July 2, August 2, September 2, October 2, November 2, December 2.

236.

Q: Two babies are born at the same moment, but they have different birthdays. How?

A: They are born in different time zones, in different places around the world.

237.

Q: What do you call a blind dinosaur?

A: Do-you-think-he-saur-us.

238.

Q: What do you call a thousand rabbits walking backwards away from you?

A: A receding hairline.

239.

Q: What do you call a dumb bunny?

A: A hare brain!

240.

Q: What do you call a snowman in summer?

A: A puddle.

241.

Q: What do you call an old snowman?

A: Water.

242.

Q: What did the snowman say to the sun?

A: I'm too cool for you!

243.

Q: Where do snowmen go to dance?

A: A snow ball.

244.

Q: Where does a snowman keep his money?

A: In a snow bank.

245.

Q: What did the right eye say to the left eye?

A: Just between us, something smells.

246.

Q: What did one wall say to the other wall?

A: Meet you at the corner.

247.

Q: What did one blueberry say to the other blueberry?

A: Why are so blue? You have to be happy!

248.

Q: What did one flea say to the other?

A: Should we walk or take the dog?

249.

Q: What kind of mouse doesn't eat, drink, walk, or run?

A: A computer mouse.

250.

Q: What kind of suits do lawyers wear?

A: Lawsuits.

251.

Q: What kind of coat can only be put on when it's wet?

A: A coat of paint.

252.

Q: What kind of underpants do reporters wear?

A: News briefs.

253.

Q: Why did the chicken cross the road?

A: To get to the other side.

254.

Q: What do basketball players have in common with babies?

A: Dribbling.

255.

Q: What has hands but can't clap?

A: A clock.

256.

Q: Where was King Solomon's temple?

A: On his forehead.

257.

Q: What runs but never walks?

A: Water.

258.

Q: What does a triceratops sit on?

A: Its tricerabottom.

259.

Q: How deep is a frog's pond?

A: Knee deep knee deep.

260.

Q: What should you do if you find a dinosaur in your bed?

A: Find somewhere else to sleep.

261.

Q: What do you call an ant who lives with your great uncle?

A: Your great ant.

262.

Q: What do you get if you cross a duck with a firework?

A: A firequacker.

263.

Q: What do teddy bears do when it rains?

A: They get wet.

264.

Q: What do you call a crate of ducks?

A: A box of quackers.

265.

Q: What does a mixed-up hen lay?

A: Scrambled eggs.

266.

Q: Why shouldn't you tell a secret on a farm?

A: Because the potatoes have eyes and the corn has ears.

267.

Q: Why do hummingbirds hum?

A: Because they forgot the words.

268.

Q: What did one egg say to the other egg?

A: Let's get cracking!

269.

Q: What do you do if a teenager rolls her eyes at you?

A: Pick them up and roll them back.

270.

Q: Why was the man running around his bed?

A: He wanted to catch up on his sleep.

271.

Q: What's the easiest way to double your money?

A: Put it in front of the mirror.

272.

Q: When you have more of me you see less, what am I?

A: Darkness.

273.

Q: What does an evil hen lay?

A: Deviled eggs.

274.

Q: Why are elephants so poor?

A: Because they work for peanuts.

275.

Q: Where do tough chickens come from?

A: Hard boiled eggs.

276.

Q: What has eight legs and eight eyes?

A: 8 pirates.

277.

Q: What position does a ghost play in soccer?

A: Ghoulie.

278.

Q: What monster plays tricks on Halloween?

A: Prank-enstein.

279.

Q: Why didn't the mummy have any friends?

A: Because he was too wrapped up in himself.

280.

Q: What road has the most ghosts haunting it?

A: A dead end.

281.

Q: Why are vampires tough to get along with?

A: Because they're a pain in the neck.

282.

Q: What is a mathematician's favorite dessert?

A: Pi.

283.

Q: What do you call a pirate with two eyes and two legs?

A: A rookie.

284.

Q: What is brown and sticky?

A: A stick.

285.

Knock, knock

Who's there?

Double.

Double who?

W!

286.

Knock, knock

Who's there?

Mikey

Mikey who?

Mikey doesn't fit in the keyhole.

287.

Knock, knock

Who's there?

Atch

Atch who?

Bless you!

288.

Knock, knock

Who's there?

I am

I am who?

You don't know who you are?

289.

Q: What did one flag say to the other?

A: Nothing, it just waved.

290.

Q: What kind of crackers do firemen put in their soup?

A: Firecrackers.

291.

Q: What do you call a popular perfume?

A: A best-smeller.

292.

Q: When is the moon the heaviest?

A: When it's full.

293.

Q: If a dictionary goes from A to Z, what goes from Z to A?

A: A zebra.

294.

Q: If you drop a white hat into the red sea, what does it become?

A: Wet.

295.

Q: Why can't Cinderella play basketball?

A: She keeps running away from the ball.

296.

Q: What's the difference between a jeweler and a jailer?

A: One sells watches and the other watches cells.

297.

Q: What rock group has four guys who don't sing?

A: Mt. Rushmore.

298.

Q: Why do elephants never forget?

A: Because nobody ever tells them anything.

299.

Q: What is white when it's dirty and black when it's clean?

A: A blackbeard.

300.

Q: What is the capital of Washington?

A: W.

301.

Q: What did the light say when it was turned off?

A: I'm delighted.

302.

Q: Did you hear about the restaurant on the moon?

A: Great food but no atmosphere.

303.

Q: Why did the boy bury his flashlight?

A: Because the batteries died.

304.

Q: Why are giraffes slow to apologize?

A: It takes them a long time to swallow their pride?

305.

Q: What belongs to you but is used more by others?

A: Your name.

306.

Q: What has a neck but no body?

A: A bottle.

307.

Q: Two waves had a race. Who won?

A: They tide.

308.

Q: How many apples can you put in an empty box?

A: None. When you put an apple in the box it isn't empty anymore.

309.

Q: What do you get if you cross a cocker spaniel with a poodle and a rooster?

A: A cockapoodledoo.

310.

Q: Where do you send a frog to get glasses?

A: To a hoptometrist.

311.

Q: What has to be broken before you can use it?

A: An egg.

312.

Q: It's been around for millions of years, but it's no more than a month old. What is it?

A: The moon.

313.

Q: People buy me to eat, but never eat me. What am I?

A: A plate.

314.

Q: I don't ask questions but I get answers, what am I?

A: A doorbell.

315.

Q: I am an ancient invention that is still used today that allows people to see through walls, what am I?

A: A widow.

316.

Q: Why did the Easter egg hide?

A: He was a little chicken.

317.

Knock, knock.

Who's there?

Luke.

Luke who?

Luke through the keyhole and you can see!

318.

Knock knock.

Who's there?

Ice cream.

Ice cream who?

Ice cream if you don't let me in.

319.

Q: I can fly without wings and I can cry without eyes, what am I?

A: A cloud.

320.

Q: How many times can you subtract the number 5 from 55?

A: Once. When you subtract 5 from 55 it becomes 50.

321.

Q: A woman is 20 years old but only had 5 birthdays in her life. How?

A: She was born on February 29 in a leap year.

322.

Q: What has 3 feet but can't walk?

A: A yardstick.

323.

Q: What time is it when an elephant sits on your fence?

A: Time to get a new fence!

324.

Q: What did the traffic light say to the car?

A: "Don't look, I'm changing."

325.

Q: How do you make the number one disappear by adding to it?

A: Add a G and you have GONE.

326.

Q: Why did the scarecrow get a raise?

A: He was outstanding in his field.

327.

Q: What three positive numbers can be added together and multiplied together to get the same result?

A: 1, 2, and 3.

328.

Q: What's worse than a baby screaming?

A: Two babies screaming.

329.

Q: How do you know carrots are good for you?

A: Have you ever seen a rabbit wearing glasses?

330.

Q: Why didn't the lifeguard save the hippie?

A: He was too far out man.

331.

Q: A prisoner is finally released from jail. He runs around yelling "I'm free I'm free!"

A: A little girl walks up to him and says "So what I'm FOUR!"

332.

Q: Why did the computer squeak?

A: Someone stepped on its mouse.

333.

Q: What did the mother ghost say to her son?

A: Don't spook until you're spoken to.

334.

Q: What do witches race on?

A: Vroomsticks!

335.

Q: Why did the Easter bunny cross the road?

A: To prove he wasn't chicken.

336.

Q: What sport is always in trouble?

A: badminton.

337.

Q: A farmer has 10 chickens, 5 horses, 2 children and a wife. How many feet are on the farm?

A: 8. Horses have hooves and chickens have claws. Only the farmer, his wife and his children have feet.

338.

Q: What kind of dress can't be worn?

A: An address.

339.

Q: What do you wish for when you see a zombie?

A: That it's Halloween!

340.

Q: Where does a ghost go on Friday night?

A: Someplace to boo-gie.

341.

Q: What do goblins drink when they are hot and thirsty?

A: Ghoul Aid!

342.

Q: What kind of music do mummys listen to?

A: Wrap.

343.

Q: Where does Dracula keep his money?

A: In a blood bank.

344.

Q: Why do witches wear pointy black hats?

A: To keep their heads warm!

345.

Q: Where do baby ghosts go while their parents are at work?

A: Dayscare.

346.

Q: What comes at the end of Thanksgiving?

A: The letter g.

347.

Q: If April showers bring May flowers, what do May flowers bring?

A: Pilgrims.

348.

Q: Why do the pilgrims' pants always fall down?

A: Because their belt buckles are on their hats!

349.

Q: Why did the police question the turkey?

A: They suspected it of fowl play.

350.

Q: What do you get when you divide the circumference of a pumpkin by its diameter?

A: Pumpkin Pi!

351.

Q: What happened with the turkey got into a fight?

A: He got the stuffing knocked out of him.

352.

Q: What do you have in December that you don't have in any other month?

A: D.

353.

Q: Who delivers presents to baby sharks at Christmas?

A: Santa Jaws.

354.

Q: What says "oh oh oh"?

A: Santa walking backwards.

355.

Q: What's red and white and red and white?

A: Santa rolling down a hill.

356.

Q: What do Santa's elves do after school?

A: Their gnomework.

357.

Q: What is the fear of Santa Claus called?

A: Claustrophia.

358.

Q: Why does Santa have a garden?

A: So he can hoe, hoe, hoe!

359.

Q: What comes before Christmas Eve?

A: Christmas Adam!

360.

Q: Who gives puppies presents at Christmas?

A: Santa Paws.

361.

Q: What do you get if Santa goes down the chimney when the fire is lit?

A: Crisp Cringle.

362.

Q: What's a parents' favorite Christmas carol?

A: Silent Night.

363.

Q: What nationality is Santa Claus?

A: North Polish.

364.

Q: Why does Santa Claus like to go down the chimney?

A: Because it soots him.

365.

Q: What's the difference between the Christmas alphabet and the regular alphabet?

A: The Christmas alphabet has no-el.

CHAPTER 2

Bonus Magic Tricks!

Magical Color-Changing Balloon

Pop a balloon to reveal a balloon of a different color!

Prepare:

1. Put a balloon of one color inside a balloon of another color BEFORE blowing it up. Then blow up the balloons. As you blow up the inside balloon some air will get between the 2 balloons.
2. Tie the balloons at the bottom to keep the air in.
3. Use tape or wax to attach a thumbtack to your thumb.

Perform:

1. Hold up the balloon so your audience can see the color. Tell them you're going to magically turn the balloon into another color!
2. Use your thumb to secretly pop the outside balloon revealing the second balloon inside.

A Baffling Banana Trick

Peel a banana to find it is already sliced!

Prepare:

1. Get a ripe banana, a needle, and piece of thread about 18 inches long.
2. Thread the needle and poke the needle and thread into the banana just through the skin.
3. Turn the needle so it goes along the inside of the banana skin and the outside of the banana.
4. Push the needle back out of the banana skin partway around the banana and pull the thread through.
5. Put the needle back in the same hole and pull the thread further around the banana and back out the skin. Continue until the thread is going the whole way around the banana.
6. Poke the needle back out the first hole.
7. Pull the thread out the hole to slide the banana inside the skin.

Perform:

1. Show your audience the unpeeled banana, making sure they see that the banana skin has not been cut.
2. Tell them you have magically sliced the banana inside the skin
3. Peel the banana to reveal the sliced banana inside!

Pick a Card, Any Card

Magically identify the card your volunteer picked.

Prepare:

1. You will need a deck of cards, a table, and a volunteer who will help you with the trick.
2. Practice sneaking a peek at the bottom card without other people noticing.

Perform:

1. Ask your volunteer to shuffle the deck of cards.
2. Take the deck of cards back and sneak a peek at the bottom card as you put the deck face down on the table. Remember the card you saw!
3. Cut the deck in half and make 2 piles of cards. Put the new pile of cards to the right of the original deck.
4. Ask your volunteer to pick to top card from either pile and look at it but make sure you can't see which card it is.

5. Ask your volunteer to put the card face down on the top of the new pile of cards.

6. Say you're going to bury the card in the middle of deck.

7. Pick up the pile of cards on the left and put it on top of the pile of cards on the right – now your volunteer's card is somewhere in the middle of the deck.

8. Flip the deck of cards over and fan them out along the table

9. Find the card you saw at the bottom of the deck. Your volunteer's card should be right UNDER the one you saw at the bottom of the deck.

10. Hold up your volunteer's card and ask "is this your card?" Watch your volunteer be amazed at your trick!

A Needle and A Balloon

Put a needle through a balloon without popping it!

Prepare:

1. Get 2 balloons, a roll of scotch tape, and one long thin sewing needle.
2. Blow up the 2 balloons.
3. Put 1 balloon aside.
4. Put a small piece of scotch tape on each side of the balloon. Make sure the tape on one side is exactly across from the tape on the other side. The needle needs to go through the tape on both sides.

Perform:

1. Tell your audience you will magically put a needle through a balloon without popping it.

2. Hold up the first balloon (the one without the tape) and show your audience it is a regular balloon.

3. Show them the needle and explain it is a regular needle that is very sharp. To make your point, poke the first balloon with the needle and pop it!

4. Now, get the second balloon (the one with the tape on it). Tell your audience that this balloon is just like the last one they saw.

5. Say some magic words to prepare the balloon for the needle to pass through it.

6. Hold up the balloon and push the needle gently through the tape on one side. Show your audience that the needle is sticking into the balloon.

7. Gently push the needle through the tape on the other side of the balloon. Show your audience that the needle is now the whole way through the balloon.

8. Watch your audience gasp in amazement!

9. Pull the needle the rest of the way through the balloon.

10. Use the needle to pop the balloon showing the audience it is just a regular balloon.

Four Kings

The 4 kings are placed in different places in a deck of cards, and then magically appear all together at the top of the deck.

Prepare:

1. Get a regular deck of cards.
2. Find the 4 kings.
3. Select 3 other cards from the deck and put them behind the 4 kings. You will be showing the kings, and you will keep these 3 cards hidden behind the 4th king.
4. Keep the rest of the deck handy.

Perform:

1. Hold up and fan out the 4 kings for your audience to see. Keep the 3 other cards hidden behind the last king.

2. Put the 4 kings face down on top of the rest of the deck. Now the 4 kings will be buried under 3 other cards.

3. Tell your audience a story about the 4 kings so you can put them in random places of the deck.

4. Explain that once upon a time there were 4 kings who lived in 4 different lands.

5. Say that one king lived very far away, so far that it would take 7 days by horse to meet his friends. At the same time, take the top card from the deck (don't let your audience see it) and push it into the deck near the bottom so that it disappears into the deck.

6. Say that another king lived closer, but it would still take 3 days to ride and visit his friends. At the same time, take the next card from the top of the deck and push it into the middle of the deck.

7. Say that the 3rd king lived right in between the first 2. Take the next card from the top of the deck and put it right in between where you

put the first card and where you put the second card. Push it into the deck so it disappears.

8. Then say that the 4th king stays just where he is which is a few days ride from his friends. Pick up the next card from the top of the deck, which is actually the first King card and show it to the audience.

9. Then continue the story and say that luckily for the 4th king, his friends all come to visit him and he doesn't have to ride anywhere at all. Put the deck face up on the table and show all 4 kings are together at the top of the deck!

DEDICATION

For Abby, Owen, Ellie, Natalie, and Amanda who keep us laughing every day of the year.

Made in the USA
Middletown, DE
16 December 2019